everyday
WARRIOR

The Action Guide for
ordinary people who
desire extraordinary results

FRANK GIGANTE

Everyday Warrior

For information regarding permission, write to:
The Zebra Ink
publisher@thezebraink.com
The Zebra Ink, 410 Simpson Road, Rochester, NY 14617
www.thezebraink.com

Printed in the United States of America

Copyeditor: Virginia Kennedy-Tette
Cover Design: Michelle Radomski
Interior Formatting: OneVoiceCan.com

DEDICATION

When I first began my weekly mantras it was intended to motivate and inspire others and to share the positivity and wondrous mindset through which I see life, and the limitless possibilities of what we are truly capable of doing in our lives.

My daughters were young when this began. As they grew I found myself sharing more of these mantras with them as they faced obstacles and experiences in their lives thinking they could use a different perspective or an uplifting thought.

This book, my first adventure into published works, is dedicated to my daughters, so they may read and explore these pages and always know that anything is possible. To let them know, they are only limited by the restraints they create within their own minds when they doubt their abilities, their passion, and their drive to achieve great things and dream even bigger dreams.

To Gabriella and GinaMarie, may you always dream big, know anything is possible if you are willing to go after it. No matter what obstacles may seem in your way, and no matter how many times you may get knocked down along the way, you always have the strength, the courage, and the intellect to get back up and to "Rise and Conquer."

TABLE OF CONTENTS

INTRODUCTION

Everyday Warrior! That is what you are. Everyday warriors are not heroes or giants that you would typically describe. They are the ones who get up everyday, with a vision of what must get done and they set their actions in motion to accomplish those goals. It isn't always glamorous. It isn't about posting the greatest selfie on Instagram or social media. Nope. The Everyday Warrior handles his or her business in private—head down, focused and grinding day after day in pursuit of something better. There is greatness within the Everyday Warrior and it is this relentless pursuit to become someone more than he or she is now that drives them to get up each morning and fight to accomplish their goals.

"Success doesn't happen by accident. You make it happen. But before you reach that road to victory, some things about yourself have to be changed." — Kevin J. Donaldson

Mindset, habits, and routines build success. You are in complete control of these aspects of your life and thus, you determine your success. This guide is the first step in changing or creating a shift in your mindset and in your actions.

As George Harrison once sang, "If you don't know where you're going, any road will take you there." To accomplish anything, whether it is cleaning a room or building a house, there needs to be a plan in place. One must know the steps of the process as well as the order in which those steps need to be completed. Laid out in the pages of this book are the tools to build the road map needed to achieve any and all of your goals—from the smallest task to your grandest dream. All require a plan, a map, and a defined process. It is not the goals that ever need to be scaled down, but simply put, it is the plans and actions that must change to continue moving forward to meet the goal.

Goals are achieved through discipline. Discipline is learned through time and experience. When I was younger, it was my dad who worked to instill discipline in me when it came to lifting weights. He was the one who bought me my first weight set as a birthday gift. My dad helped me set up a schedule and would frequently keep me on track. As a 14 year old high school freshman, my goal was to increase my fitness to improve as a gymnast and also for overall health. Like any 14 year old teen, my interests were varied and lifting was not always my focus or priority. My dad instilled the consistent commitment and work ethic needed to make those qualities intrinsic. It was the beginning of the journey.

A few years down the road in my late teens, I was very much into lifting and even more competitive bodybuilding. The discipline to do what I had to do to step on stage was now coming from within me. I had a few people who helped me prepare for those first shows, but I had to take it upon myself to stick to a plan, to get to the gym, eat my meals as planned and practice posing. I am sure it wasn't the most efficient or effective plan, but I was doing what I knew at that time and saw it through with my full attention. The process continued.

Over the years, I further utilized and refined the tools and techniques I had gained and applied them to various areas of life from completing a college degree, a master's degree, starting a career, learning woodworking as another hobby and passion, and the list goes on. When it came to my competitive career as a drug free bodybuilder, I had stopped competing shortly after college as my priorities shifted towards finding and beginning a career. I still trained as hard as ever and the passion and dreams were fully alive, but competing was not my focus. Fast forward 15 years later. I wanted to get back into competitive bodybuilding and turn dreams into reality.

I started with what I knew. I had the notes and plans I once used many years before and those became the blueprint. I updated those with the 15 years of knowledge and science that I gained over that time, and soon stepped back on stage. Within several years, not only was I competitive in my class, but I earned a pro card, making the dream of a 16–18 year old teen a reality. That, however, was only the beginning. To compete with some of the best professional natural bodybuilders in the world requires a whole other level of discipline, focus, and attention to details.

With every competition and experience, I gained knowledge to further refine my skills and habits, to be not only a better competitor, but also a better person. This process of setting goals, overcoming obstacles, holding myself accountable, and working as efficiently and intelligently as I do intensely, carries into every area of my life, not just bodybuilding.

I want share my experience and effective strategies with others. For years I have been helping people gain control and take charge of their goals, whether it be fitness and nutrition related, or in some other area of life. That has led me to giving seminars and presentations to share my strategies and influence others to follow their own passions and paths. The next step is writing this guide to help more even more people.

We are the Everyday Warriors. We have small goals, tasks, and challenges that we face everyday. No one is there to cheer us on. There are no cameras and no fanfare. Yet, we get up each day and do what needs to be done to keep moving forward. Some days are better than others. I believe that with this motivational planning guide, you will become even more aware of your own power to take action and move forward. Those "not so great days" will become fewer and farther between. You will have better clarity. You will block out the distractions. You will no longer let roadblocks and setbacks define you or stop you. Rather you will see them as opportunities to become stronger, better, and who you know you truly could be.

Thank you for purchasing this guide. Thank you for being an Everyday Warrior! Thank you for choosing to make a change and do something different so that you may start getting different results; better results; and yes, desired results.

Rise and Conquer—

Frank Gigante

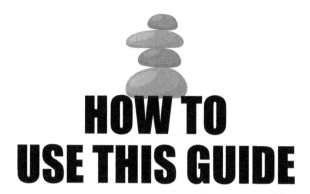

HOW TO USE THIS GUIDE

MIND MAPPING PAGE

Before the week begins, use the mind mapping page to get ideas and thoughts down on paper. There may be no rhyme or reason to these thoughts, just a place to get thoughts out of your head. One of the greatest obstacles to accomplishing anything is having too many decisions to make about what actions to take first. Getting things out on paper releases that tension, clears the mind, and then enables one to better prioritize how best to act and in which order to proceed.

WEEKLY GOAL

For example, there are times when I know I have several hours in which to accomplish a "to-do" list. If I start rattling all the things off in my head, from doing dishes to mowing the lawn, to getting in a cardio workout, writing, house projects, etc ... I would become paralyzed by having too much to do and unsure what to do first. With it out of my head and in visual form, it becomes much easier to pick one thing and start.

Starting is the key. No matter what the task is, it only grows larger as it weighs on us from inaction. Once you start, the process of action is in motion, the wall is broken, and the fears and anxiety dissipate. Those unknowns and mental roadblocks that kept you from doing a task are replaced with knowledge and experience. With that real-life feedback you can then map out our next course of action, with confidence and certainty rather than fear.

From your finished mind map decide what it is you can do this week. Consider these questions as you dial in what specific actions you can take this week to move towards or accomplish your goal:

What can you do this week?

If your goal is run a marathon and you have never run before, you may not start out running a mile, but this week you can run around the block X number of times.

When can you do it?

If you are not going to get up at 5 am, do not fool yourself into thinking this is the week you are going to do it. You are only setting yourself up for failure ... subconscious sabotage! Schedule your actions for a time you know you can block out and commit to doing it.

When creating your action plans for each week you have to use what you have and know where you are now, in order to take realistic steps.

For example: If this will be my first week of running for any type of purpose, I may not know how far I can run in one session. I am guessing it may not be very far. My goal on day 1 might be 1–3 times around the neighborhood. If I can do 3 fairly easily, I may do another lap around until I feel I have had a sufficient and successful outing. I can use that to better plan the rest of my week. On the flip side if I set out on day 1 saying I am going to run 5 miles, I have probably set myself up for failure which is only going to have compounded effects on my mental mindset if I don't complete 5 miles.

FIRST STEP

With your goal for the week set, look to be even more precise and specific with your action steps. What will be your first action? Commit to it. Perhaps it is to pack a healthy meal for lunch. Pack this the night before. Mission accomplished and then you can build upon it.

The First Step box should be that thing that needs to happen in order for you to start and keep moving forward. What is the one action that can alleviate the biggest excuses you tell yourself as to why you haven't pursued your goal yet? It is that action that needs to be your first step.

THE ACTION STEPS TABLE

The Action Steps Table is a visual guide to what else you will commit to accomplishing this week. At the end of the week, it comes down to a simple question ... either you did it and held yourself accountable or you did not take action and have made no progress this week.

REFLECTIONS SPACE

Use this space during the week as well as at the end of the week to jot down some thoughts and notes about what you did do, what you learned or gained, as well as how you can improve or build upon this week's successes in the upcoming week or weeks.

Likewise, if something didn't go well, or you didn't finish what you said you would this week, you may jot down some thoughts as to what kept you from them and then how to overcome those obstacles in the coming week.

During the week you may have ideas of what you want to do next and there is space to jot those ideas down as well. They may be immediately applicable actions for the following week or just plans for down the road. Either way they are valid and should be written down, so they are not forgotten.

This guide is meant to be interactive and an ongoing work. As you focus on goals, commit to action, and build upon each and every success you will create on your journey. This book is not just about planning goals and working to accomplish them.

"Every different level of your life will require a different you."
— *Author Unknown*

The journey is necessary and where the real growth and rewards are to be discovered. This book is one of transformation. Where you are when you start is not the same person you will be in a year, when you have filled the pages of this book and have accomplished large goals by consistently meeting and exceeding your own expectations and limits. The journey will bring about changes, self-discoveries, letting go of past restraints, and building a confidence and attitude that empowers you to become the person you truly want to be and are meant to be.

WEEK 1

"All our dreams can come true,
if we have the courage to pursue them."
— *Walt Disney*

What a great time to focus on a dream and the actions needed to make it a reality. Dreaming is the easy part. It is going to take dedication, commitment, and an incredible amount of work to make it happen. All of the effort and focus you put in is what will make achieving your dream that much greater a reward. Set your sights high and begin to start the climb to make your greatest dreams a reality.

MIND MAP

WEEKLY GOAL

What is it you will accomplish this week to move closer to your larger goals? What can you do?

When will you execute your actions?

FIRST STEP

What do you need to be able to remove all excuses this week?

ACTION ITEMS

Actions: ✓ Completed:

- _____ ❏

- _____ ❏

- _____ ❏

- _____ ❏

REFLECTIONS

WEEK 2

"Persistence and resilience only come from having been given the chance to work through difficult problems."
— *Gever Tulley*

Persistence is the key to success. However, success does not come easy. It takes work. You will struggle. You may know what you want, but not always the best way or best plan to get there. It takes time to develop a solid plan. That is OK. Just like success doesn't just come to you overnight, neither do the plans, practices, and behaviors that you must follow to achieve that success. You stumble; you fall; you use trial and error to determine what works best and what doesn't work at all. All of this is necessary. Do not give up. Whether the goal is to improve your health, work towards a degree, or develop a more productive routine, it is all a process that is a necessary part of the journey. It is never instant. You may struggle, but that is just a challenge to see how badly you want it and how hard you are willing to work. Be persistent and determined this week. It is part of the path to your success.

MIND MAP

WEEKLY GOAL

What is it you will accomplish this week to move closer
to your larger goals? What can you do?

When will you execute your actions?

FIRST STEP

What do you need to be able to remove all excuses
this week?

ACTION ITEMS

Actions: ✓ Completed:

- _____ ❑

- _____ ❑

- _____ ❑

- _____ ❑

REFLECTIONS

WEEK 3

"The excuses you are making provide support for your limitations."
— Gregg Swanson

You have goals. Your largest goals are perhaps just a bit beyond you, and a bit scary. That doesn't make them impossible to achieve. You just need to break that goal down into smaller increments and more manageable checkpoints along the way. Excuses are too easy to come by. But Gregg is right—excuses offer support and become our defense for not going after and accomplishing what we really want to accomplish. Do not buy into your excuses. Find a way to keep moving forward. Break that ultimate goal down. Conquer each small step and build the foundation and momentum to reach the goals you truly want to achieve. No goal is too big. No excuse is valid enough. You can accomplish anything.

MIND MAP

WEEKLY GOAL

What is it you will accomplish this week to move closer
to your larger goals? What can you do?

When will you execute your actions?

FIRST STEP

What do you need to be able to remove all excuses
this week?

ACTION ITEMS

Actions: ✓ Completed:

- _____ ☐

- _____ ☐

- _____ ☐

- _____ ☐

REFLECTIONS

WEEK 4

"Our greatest weakness lies in giving up.
The most certain way to succeed
is always to try just one more time."
— Thomas A. Edison

Persistence. This is what leads to success. You can expect to get to the point of wanting to give up, of not knowing what else you can do. That is when you must decide to keep going. The truth is your dreams and your journeys—they should scare you a little bit. They are not going to be easy. You must put in the work, focus, and fight harder than you thought possible. It is in those moments you will realize: you can do it. You are doing more than you thought you could and as tough as this moment is, you cannot and will not give up. You must decide to try one more time.

MIND MAP

WEEKLY GOAL

What is it you will accomplish this week to move closer
to your larger goals? What can you do?

When will you execute your actions?

FIRST STEP

What do you need to be able to remove all excuses
this week?

ACTION ITEMS

Actions: ✓ Completed:

- _____ ❏

- _____ ❏

- _____ ❏

- _____ ❏

REFLECTIONS

WEEK 5

"You gain strength, courage, and confidence by every experience in which you really stop to look fear in the face. You must do the thing which you think you cannot do."
— *Eleanor Roosevelt*

If you face your fear, you often learn at least two things: First, the fear of your fear was actually greater than confronting the fear itself, and second—you are a hell of a lot stronger than you thought you were. Do not be paralyzed by your own fear. It only exists within the confines of your mind. Face it. Conquer it. Learn and grow from it, but do not let it keep you frozen in one place. Always move forward. Nothing, not even your own fears, should be given the power to stop you!

MIND MAP

WEEKLY GOAL

What is it you will accomplish this week to move closer
to your larger goals? What can you do?

When will you execute your actions?

FIRST STEP

What do you need to be able to remove all excuses
this week?

ACTION ITEMS

Actions: ✓ Completed:

- _____ ❑

- _____ ❑

- _____ ❑

- _____ ❑

REFLECTIONS

WEEK 6

"All our dreams can come true,
if we have the courage to pursue them."
— *Japanese Proverb*

As I prepared for my first set of squats yesterday, the words of a popular quote raced through my mind, "Your mind will quit a thousand times before your body does." I was determined to control my mind and make sure I pushed it past any limits or fears it would present. With that thought, squatting and the rest of our leg workout was conquered. Fear can stop you in your tracks. Be stronger than your fears. Control and conquer your mind and you can accomplish the greatest of goals.

MIND MAP

WEEKLY GOAL

What is it you will accomplish this week to move closer
to your larger goals? What can you do?

When will you execute your actions?

FIRST STEP

What do you need to be able to remove all excuses
this week?

ACTION ITEMS

Actions: ✓ Completed:

- _____ ❑

- _____ ❑

- _____ ❑

- _____ ❑

REFLECTIONS

WEEK 7

*"Whatever the mind of man can
conceive and believe, it can achieve."*
— Napoleon Hill

When you can lay self-doubt and fear aside, you find your true dreams and greatest goals. They are scary and the challenge to achieve them can be daunting. Good. Know achieving them is entirely possible. You can do it. You can do anything. The ability to do so lies in the mind. Convince your mind that you can, and then work to make it happen.

MIND MAP

WEEKLY GOAL

What is it you will accomplish this week to move closer to your larger goals? What can you do?

When will you execute your actions?

FIRST STEP

What do you need to be able to remove all excuses this week?

ACTION ITEMS

Actions: ✓ Completed:

- _____ ❑

- _____ ❑

- _____ ❑

- _____ ❑

REFLECTIONS

WEEK 8

*"If you are not willing to risk the unusual,
you will have to settle for the ordinary."*

— Jim Rohn

To do more than you once thought you could achieve and to be more than you once thought possible, you must continue to challenge yourself and take a risk just outside of your comfort zone. Attempt more than you have before. Never settle or rest on what you have already done. Push further. There are no limits. Continue to raise the bar and be extraordinary.

MIND MAP

WEEKLY GOAL

What is it you will accomplish this week to move closer
to your larger goals? What can you do?

When will you execute your actions?

FIRST STEP

What do you need to be able to remove all excuses
this week?

ACTION ITEMS

Actions: ✓ Completed:

- _____ ❑

- _____ ❑

- _____ ❑

- _____ ❑

REFLECTIONS

WEEK 9

*"A hero is an ordinary individual who finds
the strength to persevere and endure in
spite of overwhelming obstacles."*
— Christopher Reeve

Be your own hero. You don't need to impress others or fly like superman. You want to amaze yourself by doing something that you thought you couldn't do. Find it in yourself to take on something challenging; Something you want to accomplish; Something that will test your resolve and inner strength, and then fight to make it happen. Eat better. Train smarter. Start something. Finish something. Reach farther. Do more. Be more. There is nothing you cannot do. Dream bigger until it scares you. Accept the challenge and then conquer it.

MIND MAP

WEEKLY GOAL

What is it you will accomplish this week to move closer to your larger goals? What can you do?

When will you execute your actions?

FIRST STEP

What do you need to be able to remove all excuses this week?

ACTION ITEMS

Actions: ✓ Completed:

- _____   ❑

- _____   ❑

- _____   ❑

- _____   ❑

REFLECTIONS

WEEK 10

"Never let life impede on your ability to manifest your dreams. Dig deeper into your dreams and deeper into yourself and believe that anything is possible, and make it happen."
— *Corin Nemec*

If you don't go after what you want, you will never have it. If you give 50% effort than you can expect to only achieve 50% of your goals and dreams. Believe in yourself and surround yourself with people who believe in you and want to see you succeed; those that will build you up and not tear you down. Decide what you want and then proceed to make it happen!

MIND MAP

WEEKLY GOAL

What is it you will accomplish this week to move closer
to your larger goals? What can you do?

When will you execute your actions?

FIRST STEP

What do you need to be able to remove all excuses
this week?

ACTION ITEMS

Actions: ✓ Completed:

- _____ ❏

- _____ ❏

- _____ ❏

- _____ ❏

REFLECTIONS

WEEK 11

"When all your efforts are channeled through a common canal for progress, no condition can alter a single sentence of your success story! Dream it; Drive it; Be in focus!"
— *Israelmore Aylvor*

If you can dream it, you can be it! Don't let any negativity from yourself or from others deter you from reaching your greatest dreams. Believe you can and then work to make it happen! You will have to work for it, but the harder the work, the sweeter the reward!

MIND MAP

WEEKLY GOAL

What is it you will accomplish this week to move closer
to your larger goals? What can you do?

When will you execute your actions?

FIRST STEP

What do you need to be able to remove all excuses
this week?

ACTION ITEMS

Actions: ✓ Completed:

- _____ ❑

- _____ ❑

- _____ ❑

- _____ ❑

REFLECTIONS

WEEK 12

"Got an idea to start," "Thinking to start" and "Making a commitment to start" is one aspect of life.

Actually "starting" what you truly want to do in life, is a completely different ball game."
— *Manoj Arora*

The largest step to take is always the first one. It is often the fear of taking action that prevents many from ever getting out of the planning and thinking stages. It is absolutely necessary to take that leap of faith and not be stopped by your fear. You must start in order to move forward, improve, experience, learn and reach new heights. Think, plan, and then start. Take action and don't look back today!

MIND MAP

WEEKLY GOAL

What is it you will accomplish this week to move closer
to your larger goals? What can you do?

When will you execute your actions?

FIRST STEP

What do you need to be able to remove all excuses
this week?

ACTION ITEMS

Actions: ✓ Completed:

- _____ ☐

- _____ ☐

- _____ ☐

- _____ ☐

REFLECTIONS

WEEK 13

"Success is the sum of small efforts,
repeated day-in and day-out."
— Robert Collier

You can do and achieve anything, but you cannot do everything at once. You can however, do something, maybe even a few things, each day that is going to move you closer to achieving and exceeding your goals. Do not focus on what is not done yet. Focus on what you can do and put in the work today. The past is finished. The future doesn't count yet. What matters most is you break through the excuses, focus on today and put your energy into building upon yesterday's successes. Little by little these efforts will add up to great changes, new heights, and noteworthy accomplishments. Make it happen.

MIND MAP

WEEKLY GOAL

What is it you will accomplish this week to move closer
to your larger goals? What can you do?

When will you execute your actions?

FIRST STEP

What do you need to be able to remove all excuses
this week?

ACTION ITEMS

Actions: ✓ Completed:

- _____ ❑

- _____ ❑

- _____ ❑

- _____ ❑

REFLECTIONS

WEEK 14

"If you always put limits on everything you do, physical or anything else, it will spread into your work and into your life. There are no limits. There are only plateaus, and you must not stay there, you must go beyond them."
— Bruce Lee

The limits you set are only in your mind. Pushing beyond those limits is hard work. It is a mental battle to be stronger than your excuses and to confidently know that you can accomplish the greatest of goals. It will take time. It will take a solid plan. With consistent and focused effort, it is possible and attainable to repeatedly redefine your notion of what you are capable of and continuously achieve higher and higher goals.

MIND MAP

WEEKLY GOAL

What is it you will accomplish this week to move closer to your larger goals? What can you do?

When will you execute your actions?

FIRST STEP

What do you need to be able to remove all excuses this week?

ACTION ITEMS

Actions: ✓ Completed:

- _____ ❑

- _____ ❑

- _____ ❑

- _____ ❑

REFLECTIONS

WEEK 15

"Determination gives you the resolve to keep going in spite of the roadblocks that lay before you."
— *Denis Waitley*

There are going to be roadblocks. Know it. Accept it. Conquer it! You will get knocked down. You will feel down and out at times. Get back up. Crawl. Climb. Pause to rest, but make no mistake: You will keep moving forward. This is your mission ... your goal ... your desire. Be determined. Never settle. Never give up. Know that any given moment is that moment to start fresh and move one step closer to your goal. Always take that step! It will be worth it.

MIND MAP

WEEKLY GOAL

What is it you will accomplish this week to move closer to your larger goals? What can you do?

When will you execute your actions?

FIRST STEP

What do you need to be able to remove all excuses this week?

ACTION ITEMS

Actions: ✓ Completed:

- _____ ❏

- _____ ❏

- _____ ❏

- _____ ❏

REFLECTIONS

WEEK 16

"The test of success is not what you do when you are on top. Success is how high you bounce when you hit bottom."
— *George S. Patton*

Hitting rock bottom is a purposeful opportunity to gain clarity, perspective, and form a new plan. It is not meant to be a place to stay, but rather a stepping stone. Perhaps it will be a slingshot or trampoline, in which you stay long enough to set your sights on the next step. It can be a place to gather your strength and energy to undertake the next part of the journey. Regroup, refocus, and rise.

MIND MAP

WEEKLY GOAL

What is it you will accomplish this week to move closer
to your larger goals? What can you do?

When will you execute your actions?

FIRST STEP

What do you need to be able to remove all excuses
this week?

ACTION ITEMS

Actions: ✓ Completed:

- _____ ❏

- _____ ❏

- _____ ❏

- _____ ❏

REFLECTIONS

WEEK 17

"You cannot dream yourself into a character: you must hammer and forge yourself into one. Every successful person did what no one else was willing to do!"

— Unknown

The road to change and progress is not meant to be easy. The idea of hammering and forging yourself like shaping a hot iron is a great metaphor. It takes hard work and deliberate effort to become the person you are capable of being. It is not a matter of chance. It is a focused and consistent vision that demands more than you sometimes think is in you. Don't run from the challenge. Run to it and take it head on. It may not be conquered in one try, but that does not mean it won't be or can't be conquered. It will fall. You must be stronger and confidently determined that you will succeed.

MIND MAP

WEEKLY GOAL

What is it you will accomplish this week to move closer
to your larger goals? What can you do?

When will you execute your actions?

FIRST STEP

What do you need to be able to remove all excuses
this week?

ACTION ITEMS

Actions: ✓ Completed:

- _____ ❑

- _____ ❑

- _____ ❑

- _____ ❑

REFLECTIONS

WEEK 18

"To be your best, you must outwork
your previous best effort."
— *Frank Gigante*

You have probably heard the quote by Donald Cerrone, "To be the best, you have to beat the best." Well sometimes, the competition is not another person or team, but yourself. It doesn't matter what others are doing or not doing or where they are on their journey. You are on your own mission. The goal is to continually outwork yourself; to push yourself further. To push beyond your previous limits and achieve more than you ever thought possible. Do it better than last time. Be better than you were yesterday.

MIND MAP

WEEKLY GOAL

What is it you will accomplish this week to move closer
to your larger goals? What can you do?

When will you execute your actions?

FIRST STEP

What do you need to be able to remove all excuses
this week?

ACTION ITEMS

Actions: ✓ Completed:

- _____   ❑

- _____   ❑

- _____   ❑

- _____   ❑

REFLECTIONS

WEEK 19

"The mind is the limit. As long as the mind can envision the fact that you can do something, you can do it—as long as you really believe 100 percent."
— *Arnold Schwarzenegger*

At some point, someone had the belief they could fly. However, standing there flapping their arms like a bird wasn't going to cut it. What is it you WANT to do? You can achieve it. You just need to find a way and then put in the work. There is no clear path. Once you start, the path becomes clearer as you find what does and does not work and what will continue to push you closer to your goal. You must go through the experience in order to get there!

MIND MAP

WEEKLY GOAL

What is it you will accomplish this week to move closer to your larger goals? What can you do?

When will you execute your actions?

FIRST STEP

What do you need to be able to remove all excuses this week?

ACTION ITEMS

Actions: ✓ Completed:

- _____ ❏

- _____ ❏

- _____ ❏

- _____ ❏

REFLECTIONS

WEEK 20

*"Start by doing what is necessary, then
what is possible, and suddenly you
are doing the impossible."*
— *Francis of Assisi*

Going after what you truly want is never easy. It is not meant
to be. It is meant to challenge and test you; force you out of
your comfort zone to see how much you want it. Start small—
one action at a time. Don't wait. Don't hold back. Go after it,
but realize you are not meant to accomplish it all at once. It will
take time, effort, and persistence. But when you get to the
point you realize you are doing what once seemed impossible,
you will know it is all worth it.

MIND MAP

WEEKLY GOAL

What is it you will accomplish this week to move closer
to your larger goals? What can you do?

When will you execute your actions?

FIRST STEP

What do you need to be able to remove all excuses
this week?

ACTION ITEMS

Actions: ✓ Completed:

- _____ ❑

- _____ ❑

- _____ ❑

- _____ ❑

REFLECTIONS

WEEK 21

"Cause if you're willing to go through all the battling you got to go through to get where you want to get, who's got the right to stop you? I mean maybe some of you guys got something you never finished, something you really want to do, something you never said to someone, something ... and you're told no, even after you paid your dues? Who's got the right to tell you that, who? Nobody! It's your right to listen to your gut, it ain't nobody's right to say no after you earned the right to be where you want to be and do what you want to do!"

— Rocky Balboa

No one and nothing can stop you once you decide that you are going to go after what you want. Do not let others opinions, doubts, or lack of belief in you and your goals keep you from reaching your full potential and achieving your dreams. Make them a reality. It is not a sprint but a journey. You must believe in your own journey and fulfilling your own destiny. No one else matters in your journey because it is yours. People will support you but it is up to you to go after your dreams. Seize the moment.

MIND MAP

WEEKLY GOAL

What is it you will accomplish this week to move closer
to your larger goals? What can you do?

When will you execute your actions?

FIRST STEP

What do you need to be able to remove all excuses
this week?

ACTION ITEMS

Actions: ✓ Completed:

- _____ ❑

- _____ ❑

- _____ ❑

- _____ ❑

REFLECTIONS

WEEK 22

*"If you spend too much time thinking
about a thing, you'll never get it done."*
— Bruce Lee

Thinking about doing something is not the same as actually doing it. At some point, the thinking, planning, and guessing must end and you must take action. You don't need all the answers and details laid out to begin, but instead, begin and let the rest reveal itself through experience. Don't wait too long or overthink things. Begin and then keep going.

MIND MAP

WEEKLY GOAL

What is it you will accomplish this week to move closer to your larger goals? What can you do?

When will you execute your actions?

FIRST STEP

What do you need to be able to remove all excuses this week?

ACTION ITEMS

Actions: ✓ Completed:

- _____ ❑

- _____ ❑

- _____ ❑

- _____ ❑

REFLECTIONS

WEEK 23

"Get excited and enthusiastic about your own dream. This excitement is like a forest fire—you can smell it, taste it, and see it from a mile away."
— Denis Waitley

You must light your own fire. Focus on your passion, your dreams, your goals. Envision them becoming reality after all the work, the sacrifice, the courage, and the risk of getting out of your comfort zone. That excitement, that energy, that pride ... that is the match that ignites your fire now. Today. It doesn't matter how big your vision is or how far off it is to become reality. Every step counts. No one else can light this fire and find that passion for you. Strike the match today and let it become an inferno!

MIND MAP

WEEKLY GOAL

What is it you will accomplish this week to move closer
to your larger goals? What can you do?

When will you execute your actions?

FIRST STEP

What do you need to be able to remove all excuses
this week?

ACTION ITEMS

Actions: ✓ Completed:

- _____ ❑

- _____ ❑

- _____ ❑

- _____ ❑

REFLECTIONS

WEEK 24

"The thrill isn't in the winning, it's in the doing."
— *Chuck Noll*

The journey is much more meaningful and important than the destination. For those of you on your own journey to achieving your goals, Everyday is a battle, a stepping stone, a learning experience, and often many little victories in any given day or week. Reaching your ultimate goal is most definitely important and the driving force behind your motivation to improve. You wouldn't want it handed to you. It becomes meaningful because of all of the hard work, consistent determination, and obstacles you have overcome on your journey to reach that goal. It is in the journey that the winning lies. Keep pushing each and everyday and know that each step forward is a victory!

MIND MAP

WEEKLY GOAL

What is it you will accomplish this week to move closer
to your larger goals? What can you do?

When will you execute your actions?

FIRST STEP

What do you need to be able to remove all excuses
this week?

ACTION ITEMS

Actions: ✓ Completed:

- _____   ❑

- _____   ❑

- _____   ❑

- _____   ❑

REFLECTIONS

WEEK 25

"Every strike brings me closer to the next home run."
— Babe Ruth

Failure is success. Failure is a necessary part of your journey to succeed. Accepting that thought is an overwhelming concept. You cannot and should not wait for all the conditions to be perfect before you attempt something. The conditions will never be perfect. You must put your fears aside and attempt what you are truly after. It is in the attempting that there can be no failure. Even if you miss the mark you set, you are closer, and now wiser, than you were before you tried. Now you simply try again— but better and smarter having learned from your first attempt. Go for it!

MIND MAP

WEEKLY GOAL

What is it you will accomplish this week to move closer
to your larger goals? What can you do?

When will you execute your actions?

FIRST STEP

What do you need to be able to remove all excuses
this week?

ACTION ITEMS

Actions: ✓ Completed:

- _____ ❏

- _____ ❏

- _____ ❏

- _____ ❏

REFLECTIONS

WEEK 26

"A dream doesn't become reality through magic;
it takes sweat, determination and hard work."
— *Colin Powell*

Never give up on your dreams. The course in which you thought you would take to get there may change and may look a whole lot different than when you first started, but that doesn't mean you cannot or will not reach your destination. Be flexible in your plans and make the adjustments as you go. Do not give up on the dream. Work hard, trust the process, and continue to improve your plans as you move closer to your goals and face greater challenges.

MIND MAP

WEEKLY GOAL

What is it you will accomplish this week to move closer
to your larger goals? What can you do?

When will you execute your actions?

FIRST STEP

What do you need to be able to remove all excuses
this week?

ACTION ITEMS

Actions: ✓ Completed:

- _____   ❑

- _____   ❑

- _____   ❑

- _____   ❑

REFLECTIONS

WEEK 27

"We gain strength, and courage, and confidence by each experience in which we really stop to look fear in the face ... we must do that which we think we cannot."
— Eleanor Roosevelt

What is that "thing" that you want to do but haven't because something is holding you back? Maybe it is something small, but maybe it is something that you have never told anyone before. Why should you think you can't do something? There is no reason for that thought other than fear. As a wise, older neighbor just recently shared, "There is nothing stronger than a person." You are that strong. We all are. You just need to believe it and face your fears and accept the reality that you can do "that which we think we cannot."

MIND MAP

WEEKLY GOAL

What is it you will accomplish this week to move closer to your larger goals? What can you do?

When will you execute your actions?

FIRST STEP

What do you need to be able to remove all excuses this week?

ACTION ITEMS

Actions: ✓ Completed:

- _____ ❑

- _____ ❑

- _____ ❑

- _____ ❑

REFLECTIONS

WEEK 28

"The last thing you want to do is finish playing or doing anything and wish you would have worked harder."
— Derek Jeter

At the end of the day, you want to be able to look back and know that you did everything you could do and did it to the best of your ability. To achieve this, you need to start your day with the conviction of knowing what you want to accomplish on this day, and that you will achieve those goals. Form the plan. Execute the plan. End the day with no regrets. Today is that day. Work hard.

MIND MAP

WEEKLY GOAL

What is it you will accomplish this week to move closer to your larger goals? What can you do?

When will you execute your actions?

FIRST STEP

What do you need to be able to remove all excuses this week?

ACTION ITEMS

Actions: ✓ Completed:

- _____ ❑

- _____ ❑

- _____ ❑

- _____ ❑

REFLECTIONS

WEEK 29

"One that would have the fruit must climb the tree."
— *Thomas Fuller*

You want something? Go after it. No one can stop you. If you are willing to do the work, if you are willing to climb, then no one can take that from you. That desire, that goal, that commitment, comes from within. It is yours alone. One step at a time, you must climb. Keep going and do not stop. The fruit you can see and want from the bottom of the tree may only be the beginning of much greater fruit once you get to the top!

MIND MAP

WEEKLY GOAL

What is it you will accomplish this week to move closer to your larger goals? What can you do?

When will you execute your actions?

FIRST STEP

What do you need to be able to remove all excuses this week?

ACTION ITEMS

Actions: ✓ Completed:

- _____ ❑

- _____ ❑

- _____ ❑

- _____ ❑

REFLECTIONS

WEEK 30

"It is not the mountain we conquer, but ourselves."
— Edmund Hillary

You challenge yourself in so many ways. You put expectations and demands upon yourself and are brutal in your pursuit and efforts to reach and achieve such lofty goals. All of this goes on within you and you alone. There is no need to compare yourself to others, or their goals, efforts, and achievements—they are not meant to be equal or comparable in any way. No, your goals, and path are for you only. When you push yourself and work to achieve great things, you conquer only yourself and transform your own being into something greater—physically, mentally, and emotionally. The pursuit is worth it. Conquer!

MIND MAP

WEEKLY GOAL

What is it you will accomplish this week to move closer
to your larger goals? What can you do?

When will you execute your actions?

FIRST STEP

What do you need to be able to remove all excuses
this week?

ACTION ITEMS

Actions: ✓ Completed:

- _____ ❑

- _____ ❑

- _____ ❑

- _____ ❑

REFLECTIONS

WEEK 31

*"Victory is always possible for the person
who refuses to stop fighting."*
— *Napoleon Hill*

Victory is not defined by a trophy, a title, or a championship. Victory is personal and unique to each person on their own journey. Victory is setting large goals, keeping your own word to yourself and putting in the work consistently in order to achieve those goals. The daily challenges will be tough and overcoming them will be difficult, but by refusing to give up, that is how you become victorious.

MIND MAP

WEEKLY GOAL

What is it you will accomplish this week to move closer to your larger goals? What can you do?

When will you execute your actions?

FIRST STEP

What do you need to be able to remove all excuses this week?

ACTION ITEMS

Actions: ✓ Completed:

- _____   ❑

- _____   ❑

- _____   ❑

- _____   ❑

REFLECTIONS

WEEK 32

*"Only those who will risk going too far
can possibly find out how far one can go."*
— T. S. Eliot

The limits you set are only created in your own mind. The more you can take the risk and stretch your thoughts, ideas, dreams, and goals, the more you become capable of achieving until you start accomplishing things that were once beyond what you thought possible. Whether it is in the gym, or in life, the smallest risk can lead to the greatest reward. Consider the possibilities, prepare the plan, and take the risk to move beyond what is known and comfortable. Achieve greater!

MIND MAP

WEEKLY GOAL

What is it you will accomplish this week to move closer
to your larger goals? What can you do?

When will you execute your actions?

FIRST STEP

What do you need to be able to remove all excuses
this week?

ACTION ITEMS

Actions: ✓ Completed:

- _____ ☐

- _____ ☐

- _____ ☐

- _____ ☐

REFLECTIONS

WEEK 33

*"It is your passion that empowers you to be able
to do that thing you were created to do."*
— *T. D. Jakes*

You have a passion for something in life. Do not be afraid to go after it. Pour yourself into it. Allow yourself to recognize, feel and nurture that passion, that excitement, that adrenaline. Live it! For it is yours and yours alone. Passion!!

MIND MAP

WEEKLY GOAL

What is it you will accomplish this week to move closer
to your larger goals? What can you do?

When will you execute your actions?

FIRST STEP

What do you need to be able to remove all excuses
this week?

ACTION ITEMS

Actions: ✓ Completed:

- _____ ❏

- _____ ❏

- _____ ❏

- _____ ❏

REFLECTIONS

WEEK 34

"As you think, so shall you become."
— Bruce Lee

Mindset is everything. Whatever you want to do, be, or accomplish is possible. It all must begin with the right mindset. Knowing that you can is the first step. Accepting that it will be hard and that it will challenge you in ways you cannot predict is the next step. Ultimately you must believe with all of your being that you are capable of handling and conquering every obstacle and you will succeed beyond a shadow of a doubt.

MIND MAP

WEEKLY GOAL

What is it you will accomplish this week to move closer
to your larger goals? What can you do?

When will you execute your actions?

FIRST STEP

What do you need to be able to remove all excuses
this week?

ACTION ITEMS

Actions: ✓ Completed:

- ▪ _____ ❑

- ▪ _____ ❑

- ▪ _____ ❑

- ▪ _____ ❑

REFLECTIONS

WEEK 35

"Success means having the courage, the determination, and the will to become the person you believe you were meant to be."
— George A. Sheehan

Go after what you want and what you believe you are meant to be. Thinking about it is not enough. Believing it is not enough. Find the strength and determination, to not only create a plan, but to act on it and follow it through each and everyday. It is not easy. Some days you simply do not feel like it. But that is gut check time to find the cause. If it is an excuse, then cast it aside. Strengthen your resolve and commit to what must be done today. Be all that you are meant to be and don't let anyone, or anything stop you to the point that you do not continue to strive for it all.

MIND MAP

WEEKLY GOAL

What is it you will accomplish this week to move closer to your larger goals? What can you do?

When will you execute your actions?

FIRST STEP

What do you need to be able to remove all excuses this week?

ACTION ITEMS

Actions: ✓ Completed:

- _____ ❑

- _____ ❑

- _____ ❑

- _____ ❑

REFLECTIONS

WEEK 36

"Don't let the fear of striking out hold you back."
— *Babe Ruth*

Risk. Anything worth doing takes some form of risk. This is where the greatness lies. You must get out of yourself and out of the comfortable box you live in. There can be no in-between. Either go after it with 100% commitment, or do not do it at all. Anything less simply guarantees you will fall short. Commit to yourself. Commit to being more than you are now. Accept the risk; take the chance and go for it all!!

MIND MAP

WEEKLY GOAL

What is it you will accomplish this week to move closer to your larger goals? What can you do?

When will you execute your actions?

FIRST STEP

What do you need to be able to remove all excuses this week?

ACTION ITEMS

Actions: ✓ Completed:

- _____ ❑

- _____ ❑

- _____ ❑

- _____ ❑

REFLECTIONS

WEEK 37

"It is during our darkest moments
that we must focus to see the light."
— *Aristotle Onassis*

You often tend to focus on what you don't have which leads to frustration and discouragement. Your perspective needs to change. Each day focus on the positive—focus on the changes you are seeing, the progress you have made and the actions you have taken and accomplished each day. The rest will come in time. A positive perspective breeds positive momentum which in turn leads to positive actions and even greater positive results. Change your perspective and keep moving forward!

MIND MAP

WEEKLY GOAL

What is it you will accomplish this week to move closer
to your larger goals? What can you do?

When will you execute your actions?

FIRST STEP

What do you need to be able to remove all excuses
this week?

ACTION ITEMS

Actions: ✓ Completed:

- _____ ❏

- _____ ❏

- _____ ❏

- _____ ❏

REFLECTIONS

WEEK 38

"The most essential factor is persistence—
the determination never to allow your energy
or enthusiasm to be dampened by the
discouragement that must inevitably come."
— James Whitcomb Riley

Persist!! This is a journey that takes time, heart, consistent effort and persistence! Of course there are going to be obstacles and challenges. There are supposed to be and conquering them are what builds strength, character, pride and renewed determination. Know that you are meant to struggle; you are meant to face conflict, but also have the confidence to know that you will overcome! That is how success is created! Stay focused and keep going!

MIND MAP

WEEKLY GOAL

What is it you will accomplish this week to move closer
to your larger goals? What can you do?

When will you execute your actions?

FIRST STEP

What do you need to be able to remove all excuses
this week?

ACTION ITEMS

Actions: ✓ Completed:

- _____   ❑

- _____   ❑

- _____   ❑

- _____   ❑

REFLECTIONS

WEEK 39

*"Do not dwell in the past, do not dream of the future,
concentrate the mind on the present moment."*
— Buddha

Focus on the task at hand. There is no point in being concerned about what you have or have not done before today. That moment has passed. It is good to know where you want to go and what you want to achieve, but the time in between does not yet exist. The only moment that matters is what you do now, today. Put your focus and effort into what needs to and must be done today and each day after. The rest will fall into place.

MIND MAP

WEEKLY GOAL

What is it you will accomplish this week to move closer to your larger goals? What can you do?

When will you execute your actions?

FIRST STEP

What do you need to be able to remove all excuses this week?

ACTION ITEMS

Actions: ✓ Completed:

- _____ ❏

- _____ ❏

- _____ ❏

- _____ ❏

REFLECTIONS

WEEK 40

"The greater danger for most of us lies not in setting our aim too high and falling short; but in setting our aim too low and achieving our mark."
— *Michelangelo*

You have something inside you that scares you to think you could truly achieve it. Don't let fear or doubt hold you back from aiming high. Dreaming big and being scared is ok. You don't have to know how you will get there. You just need to know that you are capable of accomplishing your largest of goals. The path and journey will reveal the "how" along the way as you grow to become the person that will accomplish our greatest goals. Dream big. Aim high!

MIND MAP

WEEKLY GOAL

What is it you will accomplish this week to move closer to your larger goals? What can you do?

When will you execute your actions?

FIRST STEP

What do you need to be able to remove all excuses this week?

ACTION ITEMS

Actions: ✓ Completed:

- _____ ❑

- _____ ❑

- _____ ❑

- _____ ❑

REFLECTIONS

WEEK 41

"Success is a little like wrestling a gorilla.
You don't quit when you're tired.
You quit when the gorilla is tired."
— Robert Strauss

Great quote! You have your moments when you think you have done enough, or done your best. But if you have not reached your goal, then you are not done. This is the time to dig in, dig deeper, find another way and vow to keep going. You are not done until you reach the goal. Keep going this week. Make things happen!

MIND MAP

WEEKLY GOAL

What is it you will accomplish this week to move closer
to your larger goals? What can you do?

When will you execute your actions?

FIRST STEP

What do you need to be able to remove all excuses
this week?

ACTION ITEMS

Actions: ✓ Completed:

- _____ ❑

- _____ ❑

- _____ ❑

- _____ ❑

REFLECTIONS

WEEK 42

"You will face your greatest opposition when you are closest to your biggest miracle."
— Shannon L. Alder

I am sure many of you have seen the cartoon of the man digging a tunnel and stops just before he would have broken through to the other side. Reaching your goals are much the same journey. You do not always know when the next step or the next move forward, will enable you to achieve your goal or even something greater. Every positive action has played a part in getting you to that point and you must find the resolve to see it through. Do not give up. There is no such thing as failure if you do not quit. You must keep going. You must dig deeper, work harder and smarter, and continue to take positive steps of action forward. Do not let today slip by without moving forward.

MIND MAP

WEEKLY GOAL

What is it you will accomplish this week to move closer
to your larger goals? What can you do?

When will you execute your actions?

FIRST STEP

What do you need to be able to remove all excuses
this week?

ACTION ITEMS

Actions: ✓ Completed:

- _____ ❑

- _____ ❑

- _____ ❑

- _____ ❑

REFLECTIONS

WEEK 43

"Nothing can stop the man with the right mental attitude from achieving his goal."
— *Thomas Jefferson*

Be unstoppable. If you believe you can do something, you can. There is nothing that can or will stop you unless you choose to let it stop you. Simple – decide any obstacle, sticking point, setback, or tough moment will not be the end, but just a momentary test of your resolve. Regroup, recharge, do what you need to, but find a way to pick yourself up, work around obstacles, start fresh, and keep moving forward. It is all within your control, because you control your attitude. Be unstoppable today.

MIND MAP

WEEKLY GOAL

What is it you will accomplish this week to move closer
to your larger goals? What can you do?

When will you execute your actions?

FIRST STEP

What do you need to be able to remove all excuses
this week?

ACTION ITEMS

Actions: ✓ Completed:

- _____ ❏

- _____ ❏

- _____ ❏

- _____ ❏

REFLECTIONS

WEEK 44

"Everyday is a new opportunity. You can build on yesterday's success or put its failures behind and start over again. That's the way life is, with a new game Everyday, and that's the way baseball is."
— *Bob Feller*

It doesn't matter what you did or didn't do before. What you are willing to do today is what matters most and will determine your tomorrow. Capitalize on what you are doing well. Learn from what you have not and build to improve upon those areas. What are you willing to accomplish today? Take the risk. Make the time. Do it!

MIND MAP

WEEKLY GOAL

What is it you will accomplish this week to move closer
to your larger goals? What can you do?

When will you execute your actions?

FIRST STEP

What do you need to be able to remove all excuses
this week?

ACTION ITEMS

Actions: ✓ Completed:

- _____ ☐

- _____ ☐

- _____ ☐

- _____ ☐

REFLECTIONS

WEEK 45

"Never go backward. Attempt, and do it with
all your might. Determination is power."
— *Charles Simmons*

Progress lies in the attempting. Do not let the thought of a challenge or task, keep you from starting. If you don't start, you never move forward. Once you start and attempt, whatever it is you are after, you move forward. Be determined to take action. You will learn, adjust and improve from there, but you must make the effort first. Don't be frozen by fear or uncertainty, just do and move closer to your goals.

MIND MAP

WEEKLY GOAL

What is it you will accomplish this week to move closer
to your larger goals? What can you do?

When will you execute your actions?

FIRST STEP

What do you need to be able to remove all excuses
this week?

ACTION ITEMS

Actions: ✓ Completed:

- _____   ❏

- _____   ❏

- _____   ❏

- _____   ❏

REFLECTIONS

WEEK 46

"Excellence is the gradual result of always striving to do better."
— Pat Riley

Your best today is not your best ever. It may be your best up to this point, but the journey cannot end here. Not today. There is more to do; new limits to surpass, more impossible goals to be made possible. Aim high and work hard. Nothing worth accomplishing will be achieved in a single effort. It is in the small efforts each day that will challenge and transform you into the character, and vision of who you must become to make higher goals a reality. Today is not that day to stop. Be better. Do more. Outwork your previous best and continue the journey.

MIND MAP

WEEKLY GOAL

What is it you will accomplish this week to move closer to your larger goals? What can you do?

When will you execute your actions?

FIRST STEP

What do you need to be able to remove all excuses this week?

ACTION ITEMS

Actions: ✓ Completed:

- _____ ❏

- _____ ❏

- _____ ❏

- _____ ❏

REFLECTIONS

WEEK 47

"Satisfaction lies in the effort,
not in the attainment.
Full effort is full victory."
— *Mahatma Gandhi*

There is no need to focus only on the end result or goal and base your success, or failure, on that one outcome. Focus on the effort you will make today and the progress that grows a little more each day with every effort you make. Expect to be challenged and find the fire to meet and conquer those challenges. Success is in your effort. Give your best effort with everything you have today, until there is nothing more you can do. You can be proud of your progress today, knowing you have given it all you have today. Tomorrow you will be able to give even more because of the focus of your efforts today.

MIND MAP

WEEKLY GOAL

What is it you will accomplish this week to move closer
to your larger goals? What can you do?

When will you execute your actions?

FIRST STEP

What do you need to be able to remove all excuses
this week?

ACTION ITEMS

Actions: ✓ Completed:

- _____ ❏

- _____ ❏

- _____ ❏

- _____ ❏

REFLECTIONS

WEEK 48

"Don't let anybody tell you that you cannot do something. If you want to do something, as long as it doesn't harm anybody else, do it. Choose a path and work towards it to the best of your ability."
— Phil Brooks, aka CM Punk

Anything is possible, but anything worth doing takes work. You have to be willing to lay the plan, see the path and be willing to put in the consistent work to see your goals and dreams realized. Make it happen.

MIND MAP

WEEKLY GOAL

What is it you will accomplish this week to move closer to your larger goals? What can you do?

When will you execute your actions?

FIRST STEP

What do you need to be able to remove all excuses this week?

ACTION ITEMS

Actions: ✓ Completed:

- _____ ❑

- _____ ❑

- _____ ❑

- _____ ❑

REFLECTIONS

WEEK 49

"We are made to persist.
That's how we find out who we are."
— Tobias Wolff

There are things you want to do. It is in your head that you can do it. That is all it takes to see a goal as possible. To put that thought into action takes persistence. It's not always pretty; the path isn't always clear, and the work is never easy. The only way to know that it is all worth it is to go through it and keep going. Work hard. Stay focused and make your dreams a reality.

MIND MAP

WEEKLY GOAL

What is it you will accomplish this week to move closer to your larger goals? What can you do?

When will you execute your actions?

FIRST STEP

What do you need to be able to remove all excuses this week?

ACTION ITEMS

Actions: ✓ Completed:

- _____ ❑

- _____ ❑

- _____ ❑

- _____ ❑

REFLECTIONS

WEEK 50

"It is no use saying, 'We are doing our best.' You have got to succeed in doing what is necessary."
— Winston Churchill

Do what you know you must—not what you feel like or are in the mood for. Some days you have it, but some days it is just a matter of putting all feelings and emotions aside. Do what you know needs to be done and do it with every ounce of energy required for success. No half efforts. Be proud of exceeding your own expectations!

MIND MAP

WEEKLY GOAL

What is it you will accomplish this week to move closer to your larger goals? What can you do?

When will you execute your actions?

FIRST STEP

What do you need to be able to remove all excuses this week?

ACTION ITEMS

Actions: ✓ Completed:

- _____ ❏

- _____ ❏

- _____ ❏

- _____ ❏

REFLECTIONS

WEEK 51

"Happiness does not come from doing easy work but from the afterglow of satisfaction that comes after the achievement of a difficult task that demanded our best."
— *Theodore Isaac Rubin*

Forget happiness. Change that to satisfaction, success, pride, or excellence. Lasting progress takes time and great effort. There is no such thing as leaps of progress or change in an instant. The goals you set and the results you desire, will require work, struggle, more work, and persistent effort. When you arrive at your goal and have achieved a new level of who you are, the work and challenge will have been well worth it. The results will be a solid and lasting foundation to build upon as you set your sights and journey even higher.

MIND MAP

WEEKLY GOAL

What is it you will accomplish this week to move closer to your larger goals? What can you do?

When will you execute your actions?

FIRST STEP

What do you need to be able to remove all excuses this week?

ACTION ITEMS

Actions: ✓ Completed:

- _____ ❏

- _____ ❏

- _____ ❏

- _____ ❏

REFLECTIONS

WEEK 52

"We will all fail in life, but nobody has to be a failure.
Failing at a thing doesn't make you a failure.
You are only a failure when you quit trying."
— Joyce Meyer

This is a fact. Accept it. Understand that not only will you fail at things, but that you MUST fail. It is part of the process of growth. You cannot succeed without stumbling along the way. When it comes to your goals, accept that you will get off track at times. That is OK. It allows you the opportunity to reevaluate your goals and your path to achieve them. How else could you form a better path based on knowledge and experience? With this mindset, there really is no such thing as failure. Every stumbling block is a learning experience, an opportunity for growth, and a chance to become stronger and better.

MIND MAP

WEEKLY GOAL

What is it you will accomplish this week to move closer
to your larger goals? What can you do?

When will you execute your actions?

FIRST STEP

What do you need to be able to remove all excuses
this week?

ACTION ITEMS

Actions: ✓ Completed:

- _____ ❑

- _____ ❑

- _____ ❑

- _____ ❑

REFLECTIONS

FINAL WORDS

It has been my great hope and mission in putting this guide together, that over the past 52 weeks you have found great success in undertaking the journey of accomplishing goals. I created this guide to show that anything is possible through practical and efficient steps and actions. There are no magic formulas, fads or trends that will replace daily and consistent effort when it comes to achieving your own self driven success.

I hope this guide has proven to you that you are capable of all you set out to do and you can achieve all you want to accomplish. The habits formed over the past 52 weeks should not stop because you have filled the pages of this book. Success is built on repeating positive routines consistently. You have done the work. You have proven you can accomplish goals over and over in spite of any obstacles! This is who you are! This is all you!!

Continue what you have started with this action guide. Keep your positive practices in place. Look towards the future. Set larger goals. Challenge yourself and have the confidence to know you can do all you set out to do!

Let's take a moment to look back at some of the practices and action steps you have been using and are now instilled in you, whether you realize it or not.

These steps apply to any future intentions and missions you choose to embrace and fulfill.

1. You have set goals, achieved them and set even greater goals.

52 weeks ago, you took a leap of faith to put your goals down in concrete form. You showed courage to take action and do things that were out of your comfort zone because doing so meant you could accomplish what you really wanted. You were not stopped by fear. You may have been unsure. You may have felt the fear of the unknown or what others may think, but you acted anyway!! That is huge!! Be proud of that! It all starts with just one action! Week after week you have set your expectations higher and, once a goal was accomplished, you set a higher and more challenging goal.

There are no limits to the extent of your goals and passions except those which you place upon yourself. Anything is possible or not possible—it all starts in your mind! You can do this—no matter what your "this" may be! In any area of life from professional career goals to fitness and health, to organizing your kitchen cabinets: have a vision. Ask yourself, "What is it that you want? What does your finished product look like?"

2. You made time to plan ahead and hold yourself accountable to those plans.

All the planning in the world means nothing unless you execute those plans. The smallest action beats the grandest of intentions any day. It doesn't matter what it is. Just act! You have repeatedly proven to yourself that you could start something and see it through because you chose to make it a priority! It is this conviction that turns dreams into reality and you now know you are a doer—an action taker! With your vision laid out and with ideas on how to turn your thoughts into action and reality, it is time to create a timeline and overall plan. Be realistic about your goals. Anything worth doing takes work and time and you need to be accurate and honest with how much time and work you have available and ahead of you. Take into consideration the time you currently have in your schedule to devote to working on your goal. If it is 15 minutes, then decide how to make the most of those 15 minutes.

Set a time frame, keeping in mind that some goals will take months, even a year or more. The time needed to complete a goal is not a reflection of it not being attainable.

3. You attended to the details.

You learned how to be detailed oriented even if you didn't realize it. You cannot reach the top rung of the ladder with one step. You must climb, hand over hand, step by step and reach each and every rung on your way to climb higher and reach the top. Each rung represents the details and each step required an action to move you closer to the top!

From here on out,continue to be specific and set up your day, the next few days or the week ahead. You want to plan out the actions you will take, the days and times you will complete them, and then block those times out so you do not encounter excuses or conflicting priorities during those times.

4. You have consistently put in the work.

Here is your greatest tool for success—you put in the work!! You had both easy and hard weeks. You may have gotten off track here and there. Through it all, you managed to get back on track, stick to your goals and plans and get back to work! No excuses. No throwing in the towel. You got up, brushed yourself off and started again. That resilience is to be celebrated! It took grit, tenacity, and a determination to keep going. You own and have sharpened those qualities within you. Don't ever doubt whether or not you "have it in you" to accomplish something—you absolutely, 100% do!!

Now it is time to work. All the planning in the world is only valuable if you put those plans into actions. Whether you feel like it or not, know that you made a commitment to yourself and it is time to hold yourself accountable. Later will not come. The time will pass no matter what, so make the time count and do what you told yourself you would do. When you have completed the task at hand, you will not regret doing it. You will have proven to yourself that you could and did. You will have laid one more brick in the foundation on which to build upon.

5. Acknowledge your progress.

Who you are now is not who you were when you started this journey 52 weeks ago. That is a great thing to be celebrated!! You have grown, changed and transformed! The journey has been significant and perhaps more important than the destination. Celebrate that journey!! Take a moment to look back just to see how far you've come. Have the confidence to know that wherever your journey takes you from here, you will grow into the person needed to reach your next level.

Success is not earned only when you have reached your highest goal. Success is not a trophy or an award to be displayed on the mantel. Success comes in the process of working towards your goal. Every positive action is success. It may be a stepping stone to the next level of success, but each level is necessary and each completed action is essential to the process. Take the time every once in a while to look back at where you started from, how much you have learned, done, changed, and be proud of where you are now. Someday this point too will be one more stepping stone towards a greater level of success. Be proud of what you have done, what you are doing, and where you are heading! You are who you want to become!

Rise and conquer Everyday Warrior!

ABOUT THE AUTHOR

Frank Gigante is in every way an Everyday Warrior. His never-say-quit attitude has served him well as a Rochester City School teacher, a world class athlete competing in All-Natural Professional Bodybuilding Competitions, a single father to two beautiful daughters, a brand ambassador, magazine columnist and hobby furniture maker and woodworker in his spare time.

Frank lives the virtues of this book in his everyday life. Otherwise he would never be able to accomplish all that he does. Whatever goals Frank sets, his voracious appetite to be more than he was the day before drives him to succeed. He applies the lessons he has learned throughout his life and from the Mental Strength Coaching certification course particularly when preparing for his next World Championship Bodybuilding Competition.

Frank makes it easy to follow his time-tested practices. Be sure to connect with him on his Frank Gigante Natural Pro facebook page, Instagram, Twitter and his blog on frankgigantenaturalpro.com. If it is inspiration, honesty and encouragement you are looking for, Frank delivers without fail.